Toad in the Boat

by Donna Taylor

Illustrated by Steve Haefele

SCHOLASTIC INC.
New York Toronto London Auckland Sydney
Mexico City New Delhi Hong Kong Buenos Aires

Clifford helps
Emily Elizabeth make a
castle and a moat.

The boat can float in the moat.

Vaz comes by and says, "Hi! I have a toad. He was hopping near the road."

"He's nice," says Emily Elizabeth.

Vaz puts the toad on the sand.

A foamy wave gets Vaz wet.

The toad gets wet, too.

He hops into the boat that floats in the moat.

The toad puffs his throat to croak.

"Croak! Croak! Croak!"

"He likes the boat!" says Emily Elizabeth.

"Croak! Croak! Croak," says the toad.

"His throat gets so big when he croaks," Vaz says.

"Let me snap a picture of the toad in the boat."

But –

here comes a wave!

Where is the boat?

Where is the toad?

Vaz moans, "My toad!"

Clifford finds the boat.

He finds the toad, too.

Emily Elizabeth makes a new castle.

Vaz digs a new moat.

"CROAK!"